On the cover:
The Southern facade
of the villa Ephrussi
de Rothschild
looking out on
the French garden.
In the background
the Mount Vinaigrier.
Photo: G. Véran.

Pages 2-3 and 34-35:
The patio with its
rose-colored
columns of Veronese
marble supporting
galleries
with Hispano-
Moorish arches.
Photo: R. Smith.

Above:
Aerial view of the
villa.
Photo: P. Diot.

Above:
The Southern facade
view from
the French garden.
Photo: B. Monnier.

Right page:
Béatrice Ephrussi
de Rothschild
(1859-1934).

6

PREFACE

by Marcel Landowski, permanent secretary of the Academy of Fine Arts

Among the "dream residences" the villa Ephrussi de Rothchild is one of the most enchanting. It is as though the Baroness Ephrussi de Rothchild had wanted, on the promintory Saint-Jean-Cap-Ferrat, nestled in the Mediterranean, to celebrate the harmony between art and nature. This museum which houses so many masterpieces, and these gardens that are themselves a veritable artistic creation are situated just so in this azurean setting that the result is a place of magic. The collection assembled by Beatrice de Rothschild and her husband Maurice Ephrussi are encyclopædic. All on its own the villa is a sort of Victoria and Albert museum that combines furniture and tapestries, sculptures and objets d'art, classical and modern paintings. It is one of a select club that unites the Wallace collection in London, the Jacquemert-André museum in Paris and the Frick collection in New York. The Baroness Ephrussi de Rothschild had requested in her will that her villa turned into a museum "keep the prevailing essence of a salon." Her wish was of course respected and the appeal of the resulting display testifies in favor of the history of the arts and in favor of the history of taste. This museum has succeeded in keeping the appearance of a private residence.

The villa itself can be disconcerting. Embedded into its walls, and therefore set off, are fragments from antiquity, the structure rises around a patio with a medieval colonnade and repeats Florentine and Venetian architectural themes from the XVth and XVIth centuries. This residence lyrically evokes the towns and countries cherished by the Baroness Ephrussi; Italy and Spain. It is in fact a synthesis of all Mediterranean architecture.

The villa Ephrussi de Rothschild is also a museum of gardens. Similar to the art collection that brings together works from throughout the ages and from throughout the world, the gardens surrounding the villa evoke both European and exotic landscapes recapturing the characteristics of Italian and Spanish gardens so dear to our patroness. In front of the villa, the French garden spreads out gloriously. This classical garden successfully contrasts both with the neo-Renaissance architecture of this pink-stucco residence and with the splendor of the Mediterranean greenery that bursts forth all around. It is on this peninsula of Saint-Jean-Cap-Ferrat that the Baroness Ephrussi de Rothschild was able to bring together and sing the praises of the loveliness of Creation, that of the gods and that of Man.

The visitor to the villa Ephrussi can travel through the ages and the continents in this sacred setting. He cannot but call to mind the other foundations of the Academy of Fine Arts: from the efflorescent gardens at Giverny to the Impressionists at the Marmottan museum including its Medieval and Napoleonic collections. So many places where the Academy of Fine Arts has been asked to keep the memory of great collectors and sublime creators alive. It does so with the gratitude, faithfulness and kindness of an establishment devoted to the preservation and promotion of the arts.

A PALACE BY THE SEA

The villa bequeathed to the Institut de France (Academy of Fine Arts) in 1934 by Mme Maurice Ephrussi, born Baroness Charlotte Beatrix de Rothschild (1864-1934) stands with its rose-colored walls inlaid with white marble amid a setting of uncommon perfection. Built on the narrowest part of the isthmus of the Cape Ferrat, the villa towers on one side above the inlet at Villefranche and on the other over the bay of Beaulieu. It commands a breathtaking view that stretches from the Cape of Antibes to Bordighera on the Italian coast. The mountain blends into the sea, and the pungent scent of the swamplike "garrigue" combined with the sea air and its delicate undertones haunt the gardens of the villas that line the coast by hundreds.

Admired for its beauty but also for its proximity to Nice and Monte-Carlo, the Cape Ferrat quickly attracted, during the "Belle Epoque," the attention of

the international elite who took up their winter quarters on the Riviera. In 1905 Mme Ephrussi acquired seven hectares of this terrestial paradise from under the nose of Leopold II king of Belgium who would have gladly expanded the park of his neighboring villa. It is at this point that the colossal undertaking of the villa's construction began. The rocky outcrop was to be levelled off and all of the soil and water necessary to the creation of a garden was to be brought in. This did not deter the imperious Beatrice who would stop before nothing. None could withstand her, not even the architects who followed one another at a frantic pace on the building site. Laprade, whom she summoned in 1928 for other projects, asserted in a chapter of his memoirs devoted to our demanding benefactor that eleven architects surrendered while the walls of the villa were barely off the ground. Mme Ephrussi had said to him: "I had a great number of architects (...) I had a Mr Giraud, the architect of the Petit Palais, a member of the Institut, Mr Némot, the architect of the Sorbonne, also came. But I rejected all of their projects. They were all inspected as scale models by me." Faced with such a demanding sponsor, the architect was in fact reduced to quietly carrying out orders. It is therefore not surprising to note that the conception of the villa Ephrussi discouraged some of the greatest architects. And we may say without apprehension that the real designer of the villa was none other than Mme Ephrussi herself, even if the work is officially attributed, according to Jean-Gabriel Domergue, to Aaron Messiah who conceived a number of villas on the Côte d'Azur. Elisabeth de Clermont-Tonnere wrote in 1928 in her memoirs "She has houses built and razed in the South of France, she orders groves to be displaced and commands flowers to grow during the Mistral." All things would eventually fold under her iron will. One of her contemporaries described Mme Ephrussi saying "[she is] the sort of pretty woman whose destiny it is to thwart the stupid rules of common sense." The villa on the Cape Ferrat which was built at great expense, not the least of

Above:
from top to bottom:
Nice, the English
promenade
and the jetty palace,
around 1900.
© N. D. Viollet.

The villa under
construction at the turn

of the century. The
three openings that
form the entrance to
the main courtyard
come from a 15th
century Catalan cloister.

Above center:
The patio.
Photo: R. Smith.

Above:
The villa reflected in
the basin of the
French garden.
Photo: G. Véran.

The horseshoe
shaped staircase in
the Florentine
garden overlooking
the inlet at
Villefranche.
Photo: G. Véran.

which was the captious nature of its mistress, would be her masterpiece. The construction was completed in 1912 after all sorts of mishaps, one of which almost cost the life of the villa's owner. One day during the Mistral Mme Ephrussi arrived from Paris surrounded by architects and designers who had been brought there to judge the villa and its gardens as simulated by enormous wood and painted canvas structures, when a gust of wind assailed the illustrious assembly bringing down upon them the fragile scaffolding. The fright that was caused was greater than the harm done, but everything had to be rebuilt. At this point in time Mme Ephrussi had fancied crowning her villa with two towers similar to those of the villa Medici, but she was forced to abandon the idea after seeing the lifesize model. For her residence at Cape Ferrat, Christened the "Ile de France" in memory of a cruise taken on the liner by that name, Mme Ephrussi chose a style that was inspired at once by Venice and by the Palaces at Ravenna and Florence, whence the designation *palazzino* that we find employed in the accounts of the time. The exterior walls stuccoed in pink testified to Mme Ephrussi's devotion to this color as also seen in her legendary lavatory and her villa in Monte Carlo "Rose de France". Elisabeth de Clermont-Tonnere painted her portrait saying "she was beautiful and already at the age of twenty her hair had turned white, which gave her a powdered look. She almost always wore pink dresses and seemed eternally ready to go to an elegant ball.

Mme Ephrussi sojourned little in her *palazzino* on the Cape Ferrat and ceased to live there altogether after the death of her husband in 1916, opting instead for her residences in Monte-Carlo. We do not know how the villa was furnished during her lifetime. As it is today it brings together the entire Ephrussi-Rothschild collection, this being the desire that she expressed in her will drawn up in 1933: "I bequeath to the Institut de France for the Academy of Fine Arts my villa Ile de France (...) with all of its furnishings and objets d'art and the garden that surrounds it in order to make it into a museum (...) I bequeath to this museum all of the objets d'art that I own whether they be in Paris, 19 avenue Foch, or in Monte-Carlo villa Soleil and the villa Rose de France, paintings, furniture, porcelain, tapestries, etc...

At first by birth and later by marriage Mme Ephrussi was destined to become one of the greatest collectors of this century. Daughter of the Baron Alphonse de Rothschild, governor of the Bank of France and Eleonor de Rothschild, she spent her childhood at the chateau de Ferrière where James de Rothschild had amassed one of the most sumptuous collections of paintings, tapestries and objets d'art of the time. She would keep a suite of rooms in this castle her whole life. In 1883 her marriage to Maurice Ephrussi, "Frousse" as she affectionately nicknamed him, allowed her to enter into a family of bankers and wheat exporters, originally from Odessa, who were themselves important collectors and friends of the Rothschilds. One of Maurice Ephrussi's cousins was none other than Charles Ephrussi, backer of the Impressionists who contributed to popularizing their work within the higher circles of society. Mme Ephrussi was also related to Theodore Reinach whose villa Kerylos at Beaulieu sur mer (today property of the Institut) remains one of the most magnificent evocations of ancient Greece. Within this circle of important conaisseurs, which also included Gaston Dreyfus curator of the Louvre, Edouard André or Moise de Camondo (the latter's names are still connected with two museums, those of Jacquemart-André and Nissim de Camondo) it seems that the "grand goût" was to be for them inevitable.

"He who has never known the XVIIIth century has never known the sweetness of living" said Talleyrand. Mme Ephrussi, until the end of her days, would prove Talleyrand wrong by uniting, in her various residences, the refinements of the Ancien Régime with the conveniences of her time, namely electricity and the railroad. **Jérôme Coignard**

The French garden
seen from
the loggia
Photo: G. Véran.

Above:
The Louis XVIth salon with wood ornamentation from the Crillon hotel in Paris, around 1775. In the foreground, a Savonnerie carpet made for the Louvre around 1675 and the Louis XVIth furniture.
Photo R. Smith.

Top from left to right: From the Sèvres workshop, Dutch vase with painted medallions by Pierre Ledoux, 1757; porcelain from Vincennes, 1753, porcelain cream dish in the shape of a flat shell; from Sèvres with landscape decorations and saucer with openworked edges.
Photos: G. Véran.

Right page:
Nicolas Lancret, *Bird in Flight*, around 1725, oil on canvas.

REGAL TASTE

The wooden ornamentations that line the walls of the Louis XVIth salon are attributed to Pierre Adrien Paris and come from, so it is said, the Crillon hotel. This work was part of a prestigious decor that gave out onto the former

square Louis XVth. The tapestries and furnishings are in perfect harmony and the Savonnerie carpet is privileged to come from the chapel at Versailles, the seats are upholstered with tapestries from the Beauvais workshop which was created by Louis XVIth. The attention given to the quality and origin of each object bespeaks of the choices of a great collector and can also be seen in one of the finest examples of the collection Béatrice de Rothschild, the priceless French porcelain, that abounds with pieces from Sevres and Vincennes (the other workshop founded by Louis XVIth). And Béatrice Ephrussi would have her turn to be the queen of the Riviera!
Nicolas Sainte Fare Garnot

Louis the XVth's century, which is often called the golden age of grace and elegance, took upon itself to invent new tidbits to inspire its artists. From stories of antiquity and mythology prized during the XVIIth century, there came a preference for the evocation of the refinements of daily life. Because nothing could be more gallant than to ape human beings, the fables and picturesque representations of animals became popular. You may appreciate this for yourself! Jean-Baptiste Huet, the endearing creator of the screens in the Cabinet des Singes, laid aside the fashionable trend towards the chinoiseries to dare to paint some very peculiar animals who often mime the quirks of their human masters. From Watteau to Chardin these little animals can be seen time and again, cute, loveable and sometimes monstrous, here they are depicted with levity. This light-heartedness is also present on the Meissen porcelain where the costumed animals play an unforgettable tune for us. N. S. F. G.

Left page:
detail of the panel with monkey motif attributed to Jean-Baptiste Huet. Photo: R. Smith.

Top, left to right: Porcelain clock from Wurzbourg called the "skeleton" mounted on a wild boar with oak leaf and acorn decorations, around 1750. Meissen porcelain clock with flowers, figures and parrots done in 1738.

Above:
Meissen porcelain monkey orchestra done around 1740 by the famous Kändler. Photos: G. Véran.

THE SITTING ROOM
IN THE COUNTRY

From Mme de Pompadour
to Mme du Barry,
all of the grand ladies of
Louis XVth's century
tried, within their
surroundings, to create a
new art of living:
hairstyles and costumes
became looser and
furnishings
and household objects
were adapted for
convenience's sake.
Hard lines were
abandoned in favor of
softer curves
that added to a certain
elegance and
fluidity. Béatrice Ephrussi
had no hesitations
in transposing
these eminently urbane
tendancies in her
residence on the Côte
d'Azur, popular
wintering spot.
In her sitting room that
opens out onto the garden
she could enjoy both
the refined comfort of an
interior, that one
could more easily imagine
being on the faubourg
Saint-Germain, and the
sweetness of the
Mediterranean breeze.
N. S. F. G.

Opposite:
The Louis XVth
salon with
large Aubusson
rug dating
from the time
of Louis XVth,
table for game
attributed
to Cressent
and Louis XVth
furnishings
upholstered with
Beauvais tapestries.

In the niches:
tapestries from
the Gobelins
showing scenes
from *Don Quixote*
based on
sketches by Coypel,
around 1745.

On the left wall:
Paintings
of dancers by
Frédéric Schall
(see top left)
and on the
right wall (see
above)
an oval painting
of a woman
and a young
man by François
Boucher
(photo: R. Smith).

Jean-Honoré
Fragonard,
*Woman gazing at
herself in a stream,*
wash drawing.

THE ILLUSTRIOUS FRAGONARD

Opposite, from top
to bottom:
wash drawings
by Jean-Honoré
Fragonard:
*Danae visited
by Jupiter; If he were
as faithful to me;
Farmyard.*
Below:
*Landscape with
Roman ruin,*
wash drawing
by Hubert Robert.

Top right:
pastel by
François Boucher:
Woman with rose.

Madame Ephrussi,
a lover of pastels and
drawings from the
XVIIIth century, especially
favored the work of
Fragonard. She amassed
a rare collection
of preparatory academic
studies or fantastic
subjects from various
periods of the
artist's career.
It is in this way that this
painter, originally
from Grasse, found a
refuge at the villa
Ephrussi for safeguarding
his pencil sketches
and ink drawings that he
had drafted on small
scraps of paper. What, in
fact, could be more
sensitive to the ravages
of time and light
than these ink and chalk
drawings delicately
laid out on the
pages of albums.
We may wonder
why these scraps were
so preciously
conserved to this day,
until we realize
that it is in keeping with
an unbroken
chain of fanatic
and obstinate collectors,
to whom we
are indebted. Béatrice
Ephrussi opportunely
inherited this collection.
N. S. F. G.

In the residences of
yesteryear, one
continually put oneself
foward, moving
down great reception
halls from salon
to salon. We can today
wonder if these people
were able
to enjoy any kind of
privacy? In fact
they were attributed

Above:
Madame
Ephrussi's room.
Top:
Overhang
looking out on the
inlet at Villefranche

with oval
Aubusson rug from
the end of the
XVIIIth century and
painted piers
based on
François Boucher.

Below:
Two rounded doors
framing a large
Venetian bed around
1765, covered with
Chinese silk.
(photo: G. Véran).

certain areas,
like small private suites,
where the need
to keep up
appearances could

give way to more
natural behavior.
This is reflected in the
furnishings
of the bedroom
and boudoir of Béatrice
Ephrussi. The
practical Louis XVIth
style gave these
rooms a functional aspect
all the while
everything was

arranged to add
a more personal touch
and general
intimacy to the space.
N. S. F. G.

Above:
Madame Ephrussi's
boudoir.
Wood ornamentations
from the end of the
XVIIIth century in a
Pompeian style
(see detail above,
photo: G. Véran);
desk "bonheur du
jour" by Riesener
with Marie-
Antoinette's
monogram inlaid in
bronze. On the floor,
European porcelain
dog around 1750.
Photo: B. Monnier.

ECLECTICISM:
A WAY OF LIFE

It was aboard the ocean liner "Ile de France" that Madame Ephrussi sailed the seas; and it was on a rocky outcrop, that brought to mind the cruises that she had taken, that she built her villa. During these many voyages she gathered together souvenirs from the four corners of the Earth. The Far East, a land which to some can be seen as a symbol of the illusory, offered her several of its treasures, and although

it was common among turn of the century bourgeois to find Chinese or Indian porcelain, hers were among the finest vestiges of Imperiel workmanship. She seemed to have a pronounced penchant for rare and precious objects so long as they were antique. Our own national artistic heritage, that is to say the works of the Gothic period, were as accessible to her as certain Islamic objects and ceramic tiles like those of Castelli. N. S. F. G.

Doors from the
Imperial Palace in
Peking, black laquer
and gold from
the beginning
of the XVIIIth century.
Photo: R. Smith.

Polychromatic
ceramic tile
by Castelli
with six figures
and a Virgin
and child in the sky
around 1784.

Above:
The French garden
seen from the
loggia.
The Temple of Love
at the far end
of the canal is
connected to the basin

by a stairway of
water..
Photo G. Véran.

Right page:
The hexagonal
tample in the rose
garden.
Photo G. Véran.

GARDENS OF PARADISE

The gardens of the villa Ephrussi de Rothschild are often compared to an ocean liner and it is true that their location makes this analogy all the more plausible since on either side of the elongated property swells the Mediterranean. On one side the Gulf of Eze and on the other the inlet at Villefranche. It is also true that Madame Ephrussi had a definite fancy for transatlantic cruises. To the point that some said she would oversee from the loggia, like a captain on the bridge, her thirty gardeners at work bedecked in berets with red pom poms.

These gardens are akin to the "gardens within gardens" that originated during the Roman era. The Hadrien gardens at Tivoli brought together various celebrated landmarks and monuments, and in some cases simply evoked them, or in others actually reproduced them. The evolution of this tendancy was sporadically manifest in Europe as early as the

Above, from top to
bottom: The Spanish
garden with its grotto
sheltered behind
pink marble columns,
its canal filled with
aquatic plants and
its pergola.
Photos G. Véran.

Renaissance and took hold around 1730 in England with the creation of seemingly ageometrical parks. The English influence then spread to the continent where the increasing accumulation of momuments turned some gardens into quasi-museums. These objects were coupled with plant arrangements that were meant to highlight their character. Some of the most well- known gardens in France are those of Albert Kahn, laid out from 1893 to 1905 in Boulogne on the outskirts of Paris, and those of the villa Ephrussi de Rothschild, completed in 1912. The latter was fashioned in seven years on a rocky outcrop that was entirely levelled to accomodate the estate.

In the morning when Béatrice de Rothschild emerged from the bedroom that gave out onto the west terrace, she would face the sculpted garden that at the time must have looked much different with its tufts of young, barely-grown palm trees that took up most of the ground space. The view out towards the green hillock was less clear, but the small temple based on the Trianon, crowned the cascade in the same way, the slope gave movement to the water and produced an all-over white effect, like the "water shawls" of the Orient.

At the time the flower beds constituted the most important gallery of the villa, and to create them Béatrice recruited Achile Duchêne, the landscape architect prized both in Europe and the United-States for his capacity to create gardens inspired from Antiquity.
As Béatrice de Rothschild walked forward onto the terrace she would find herself above the Spanish alcove, the first of a series of hidden gardens that one cannot see from the salons of the *palazzino*. Depending on the time of year, she could detect different perfumes, orange trees, honeysuckle, heliotrope, tuberose or thorn-apple. To arrive at the alcove she took the rounded staircase that lead her to a man-made grotto accessible by three arch-shaped openings on what was in fact the second patio of the villa.

Top:
The rock garden with its arches, fountains and sculpted rocks set amid the greenery.

Above:
The exotic plant garden with its impressive cactacae.
Photos B. Monnier.

Beyond the basin and the pergola, the Florentine alley, lined with cypress trees, took her past the rocky grotto where a marble ephebe cast his eyes away from the facing panorama, to the Japanese garden. At the time the rock garden did not exist (later the sculptures exhibited there were those that Mme Ephrussi had not found room for in her villa). She would cross the small pond using the stepping stones that lay under potsful of delicate orchids and in a few strides be in a whole new world. An exotic garden abounding with the rich foliage that luxuriated until the frosts of 1926,1956 and 1985 reduced them to a memory. She would then arrive at the rose garden the destination of her stroll. The bank was planted with a hundred different varieties of rose bushes. While a latticework of climbing roses crept up the columns that face the hexagonal pavillion.

Let us leave Béatrice to gather her roses and climb the hillock in the opposite direction. This part of the estate was called the English garden because the pine grove had been left more or less unchanged by the passage of a sinuous alley. On the other side of the ridge, the terracing of the olive trees known as the Provençal garden bespoke of the birth of neo-regionalism in gardening.

From the circular temple, which is the focal point of the villa Ephrussi, we can view the other side of the sculpted garden. The symmetry of the alleys and the shrubbery in relation to the axis of the canal seems to relate the whole to a French-style garden while the increasingly elaborate layout of the flower beds as we go towards the *palazzino*, evokes the disposition of Transalpine gardens such as the villa Cicogna in Lombardia or, relatively speaking, the Caserte Palace near Naples. French-style garden? Italian garden? Whatever the case may be they are all magician's gardens where expertly camouflaged is the obstinance and workmanship that was needed to sculpt a landscape into a veritable paradise under the canopy of heaven.
Ernest Boursier-Mougenot

Above:
Florentine alley.

Right page:
Florentine garden.

Photos B. Monnier.

Above:
View of the inlet at
Villefranche.
Photo: G. Véran.

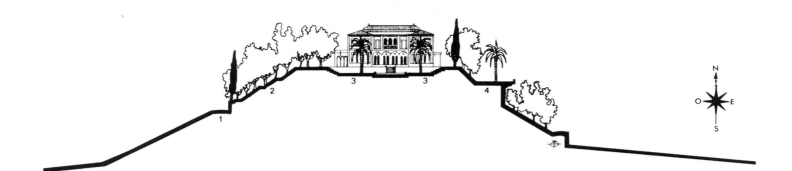

LAYOUT OF THE VILLA

1. **Gate and house of the grounds keeper.**

2. **Main courtyard with grotto-fountain.**

3. **Museum entrance.**

4. **Spanish garden.**

5. **Florentine garden.**

6. **Rock garden.**

7. **Japanese garden.**

8. **Exotic plant garden.**

9. **Rose garden.**

10. **Former English garden.**

11. **Former Provencal garden.**

12. **Temple of Love.**

13. **French garden.**

CROSS SECTION OF THE VILLA

1. **Saint-Jean-Cap-Ferrat road.**

2. **Florentine garden.**

3. **French garden.**

4. **Avenue leading to the villa.**

**Both diagrams are taken from the
Jardins de la Côte d'Azur,
1987, Edisud-Arpej.**

Above, from top to bottom: The Temple of Love overlooking the French garden, an exact replica of the Trianon.

Ceramic pagoda in the Japanese garden.
Photos: G. Véran.

PRACTICAL GUIDE

The villa Ephrussi de Rothschild is property of the Academy of Fine Arts of the Institut de France.
It is open from February 1st to November 9th everyday from 10:00 a.m to 6:00 p.m (7:00 p.m in July and August). From November 10th to January 31st on weekends and holidays (not including Christmas) from 10:00 a.m to 6:00 p.m, and during the week, from 2:00 p.m to 6:00 p.m. The visit of the ground floor salons and the gardens is not guided. The collections on the first floor are visited with a guide.

Visits are organized all year round for groups. The villa Ephrussi de Rothschild disposes of a tea room with terrace offering visitors a moment to relax in a unique setting. The gift shop offers a selection of souvenirs, post cards and books. Finally, the villa and gardens are open to receptions and seminars until 400 persons.
Villa Ephrussi de Rothschild
06230 Saint-Jean-Cap-Ferrat
Tel. : 04 93 01 33 09 -
Fax : 04 93 01 31 10
www.villa-ephrussi.com

FURTHER READING

Élisabeth de Gramont,
*Mémoires, t. 2,
les Marronniers en fleurs,*
Paris, Plon, 1928.

Paul Castella,
*la Côte d'Azur à la Belle Époque
vue par Jean Gilletta,*
Nice, éditions Gilletta, 1981.

C. White, M. Butor,
D. Allary, N. Bine-Muller,
Rêveuse Riviera,
Paris, Herscher, 1983.

Ernest J. P Boursier-Mougenot,
Michel Racine,
Jardins de la Côte d'Azur,
Aix-en-Provence, Edisud-Arpej, 1987.

André Cane,
Anglais et Russes à Villefranche-sur-Mer,
Beaulieu sur Mer,
Saint-Jean-Cap-Ferrat,
Nice 1988.

Dominique Escribe,
la Côte d'Azur. Genèse d'un mythe, Nice,
G. Vitaloni/Acam, 1988.

TO VISIT

Villa Kerylos
Discover the fascinating life
of an ancient and luxurious
Greek palace, with all its rooms,
furniture, frescoes, and mosaics.
800 m far from the Villa Ephrussi
de Rothschild, on the Beaulieu-
sur-Mer bayside.

Les numéros hors-série Beaux Arts magazine
sont édités par Beaux Arts SA.
Directeur de la publication :
Charles-Henri Flammarion.
Directeur général :
Christophe Chabloz.
Directeur de la rédaction et rédacteur en chef :
Fabrice Bousteau.
Secrétaire générale de la rédaction :
Hortense Meltz.
Maquette : Claire Luxey.
Secrétaire de rédaction : Obligée Arson.
Version anglaise : Stéphanie Berkvam.
Directeur de la création et de la fabrication :
Alain Alliez,
assisté de Marie-France Wolfsperger.
Marketing : Isabelle Canals-Noël.
Tél. 01 56 54 12 35.
Diffusion : Manon Courbez.
Tél. 01 56 54 12 32.

Beaux Arts magazine
Tour Montparnasse
33, avenue du Maine
75755 Paris cedex 15.
Tél. 01 56 54 12 34.
Fax : 01 45 38 30 01.

RCS Paris B 404 332 942.
ISSN : 0757 - 2271.
Dépôt légal : octobre 2002.
Impression : Mariogros, Turin.

Nous remercions pour l'aide qu'ils ont apportée
à la réalisation de cet ouvrage :
Bruno Monnier, PDG de Culture Espaces,
Charles-Henri Diriart, Alexis Vrousos,
ainsi que Nicolas Sainte Fare Garnot.

Left page:
The French Garden
under the snow..
Photo J. de Lestang.

Above:
The tea room.
Photo G. Véran